APOSTLES OF ANARCHY

By the same author:

V8 with PS Cottier (2022)
The Ruby Red's Affair (2022)
It's the sugar, Sugar (2021)
Acting Like a Girl (2019)
The Orlando Files (2018)
Who Sleeps at Night (2017)
One Last Border: Poetry for Refugees with Hazel Hall and Moya Pacey (2015)
Projected on the Wall (2015)

APOSTLES OF ANARCHY

SANDRA RENEW

RECENT
WORK
PRESS

Apostles of Anarchy
Recent Work Press
Canberra, Australia

Copyright © Sandra Renew, 2023

ISBN: 9780645356380 (paperback)

A catalogue record for this
book is available from the
National Library of Australia

Cover image: © Silva Vaughan-Jones
Cover design: Recent Work Press
Set by Recent Work Press

recentworkpress.com

SS

With thanks to the 1970s and 1980s

Contents

Apostles of Anarchy Chronology

1983	Milestone: Sex Discrimination Act
1990	Milestone: Brisbane Pride
1998	Milestone: No change in public drunken assaults
2020	Milestone: First Nations Land Rights continue to be publicly debated

2017	Postal survey on same sex marriage, 15 November 2017
2019	The internet is legally confirmed as an acceptable homophobic forum in pursuit of religious freedom (Israel Folau)
2020	COVID-19 in Australia

APOSTLES
OF ANARCHY

Townsville Daily Bulletin, 6 July 1978

Foreword is fore-armed

The past is alive in us, all the time. We move through and against our history, reference our own creation stories, time and time again, to our own unique experience of past events.

In Queensland in the 1980s at our end of the State, the *Townsville Daily Bulletin* referred to the demonstrators of the 80s political movements as 'apostles of anarchy'. This collection goes towards recognising the questions of separation and rage that we, gays and lesbians, 'gender diverse and gender fluid', feel still. Our experiences of being separated out from the community in the public discourse as 'undesirables', 'deviants' and 'perverts' never leaves us.

Apostles of Anarchy draws from public discourse available in national and local newspapers 1978 to 1983 and beyond.

> The archive materials are re-imagined as counter-memory and/ or resistance, counter-memories situated in opposition to official reporting. This response challenges the archive as a space that not only legitimates authorised memories but also contains bodies of fact, commentary, evidence and inference. The writing of this response is an active and conscious production of counter-memories (Webb 2021).

The protest movements (of which there were others) brought to light archives of:

- The right to march (arising from the Premier of Queensland's over-reaching response to anti uranium mining demonstrations in Sydney)
- The characterisation of Queensland under repressive public gathering restrictions as a 'police state' and police with 'Nazi powers'
- The uprising of the Lesbian movement as both part of and against the feminist movement
- Pine Gap Women's Peace Camp
- Anti-homosexual reactions to gay and lesbian teachers

I experienced these protest movements in a strangely ad hoc and disconnected sense, mainly because of a sense of being far from the hub of revolution and change which was rising in the eastern capitals and regional towns of southern Queensland. Some sense of coherence was found in a growing sense of injustice, outrage and lack of connection with the wider mainstream of the civil obedience and social acceptance young adults are expected to grow into.

In this archive-delving are some other historical articles which I have included in order to mention that the outrages of separation I felt are not unique to either me or the times. Gay men and lesbians have sociologically been border people for many years and, even now, forty years on from my decade of unease, even after decades of gains and wins in terms of community acceptance, can be made borderline again without notice. The last section is a collection representing a past manifesting in the present...although we now continue to live quietly and suburbanly, anarchy still lives in us. And, indeed, we still have thoughts of separation...

'Prohibit all street marches'

Joh Bjelke-Petersen, 1977

Part 1: Rage and the kicking in of headlights

Why our rage grows: the undoing and the doing. It's a long story. Bear with me. We lived our lesbian lives in the time just before the 'gay cancer' brought condoms front and centre to shield the queer from the rest. Even though the community was not yet mobilised in a specific fear of catching HIV AIDS and hatred for us, the deviants, rampant in the public discourse was the left-over Victorian prurience and righteous morality that had brought Oscar Wilde undone, and Queen Victoria's confusion which told us we did not exist.

It was not the Grim Reaper in the first instance, but uranium that brought about violent clashes between anti-mining demonstrators and police in Sydney. As a pre-emptive measure, the Premier of Queensland, Mr J. Bjelke-Petersen banned us from street marches, saying *don't bother applying for a permit. You won't get one*, and said the ban would apply to street marches not only in Brisbane but throughout Queensland. This brought the world closer to us in our tropical isolation. Most news seemed to happen a long way to the south, but now, the Premier brought it up to us.

'When injustice becomes law resistance becomes duty.'

Pine Gap the Images, 1983

'... a nonviolent political campaign'

The Townsville Daily Bulletin, 1978

Anarchy or duty

apostles of anarchy they called us
saying we advocated lawlessness

the march proposed is cancelled when
grapevine gossip is over-run
by news that homosexuals from Sydney and Brisbane
were bussing north to join in—
feared disruption by these militants caused the cancelling

if you take away the street,
our only expression of democracy
as a forum for dissenting, protesting, and
injustice becomes law
then our resistance becomes duty.
there were those we thought stood with us,
but unmasked as moral cowards, their cold feet went to water
the rhetoric and labelling
as *obscene parasites, lunatic fringe, the mob,*
known and unknown radicals, and *communists*
Government should know better—
when injustice becomes law, resistance becomes duty

REMOVED FROM COURT

The Townsville Daily Bulletin, 1978

Court News

refused to lower a
pink placard relating to protest
rights a young man was removed
from the ... Magistrates Court yesterday ...

A court is not a political forum [warned] the magistrate

threatened to commit him for
contempt of court

Part 2: By your names will you know us

A few months after the announcement, in January 1978, that street marching was now banned, we rode from Townsville to Minto outside Sydney on a Suzuki 350cc. I was a very mild case of 1970s 'biker'. Starting with my first bike, a yellow 100cc Suzuki, which somehow came with a matching yellow leather biker style jacket, I enjoyed a gradual progression of ever more ccs, more unnecessary and scary power, until I inadvertently did a wheel stand revving up a 10-year-old 650cc Yamaha and swapped it the next day for a beige 1970 XK Ford Falcon in 1982.

But in 1978 my girlfriend at the time was up for adventure. Neither of us had quite bargained for the more than 2000-kilometre road trip, alternating uncomfortably on the pillion. And very little of the highways, including the Pacific, the New England and the Hume, were bike friendly, so we felt every one of those rough edges, uncambered bends, blind side roads and the heavy semis that drove over us as if we weren't on the road at all. And I don't want to even think about the Queensland end of it all, which, winding through high cane was edged with innumerable blind curves and unmarked driveway entrances.

This trip was an unprepared, precipitous, bike-dyke decision to attend a Lesbian Feminist Festival, borne out of isolation and depression, even though it had been a long-held dream in bike dyke mythology to do The Big Road Trip. Sheila, a women's band and The Lean Sisters were booked for entertainment. We were out of our minds with the excitement of a women's gathering and being out and free of the repressive, antagonistic, and downright dangerous atmosphere of Townsville in Far North Queensland.

This Festival of lesbians and feminists, with its heady pride events, primed us for the March 1978 political demonstration in Brisbane where 400 women defied Bjelke-Petersen's ban on political marches and 53 women were arrested. Arrests buoyed us, we felt things were happening, changing, that we were making ourselves noticed. That our rights to be seen as participants in the community rather than observers were finally filtering through.

But then, we had to ride on back to the far north where politics were still different.

11 ARRESTED ON PROTEST MARCH

The Townsville Daily Bulletin, 1978

POLICE MAKE A CLEAN SWEEP

The Townsville Daily Bulletin, 1978

there was no violence

police make a clean sweep
    eleven arrested in protest march
a march proscribed and illegal
    charged with disobeying the direction of a police officer
arrested moments after they set out
    an inalienable right which must be defended

when police closed in [the protesters] sat on the roadway...
there was no violence
    they were released on watchhouse bail

Events occurring I

Written statement for the Magistrate from a demonstrator

I walked with my hands in the air, with all eleven of us chanting 'The Right to March, The Right to March.' As we approached the intersection a line of police moved towards us. They shouted instructions to move off the street through a loud-hailer. We all sat down on the road and continued chanting.

Two policemen grabbed my arms and pulled me up and towards the police van. They kept asking me if I was going to obey the police directive. We waited in line at the back of the van. A policewoman asked me my name and wrote it on a form. A photographer took my photo. And then I got into the van.

Events occurring II

Witness statement: Photographer from The Townsville Bulletin

I'm just beside them on the footpath as they move off down the street. One particular woman stands out. She walks with her hands in the air, all eleven of them chanting 'The Right to March, The Right to March'. They just get moving and are at the intersection when a line of police move towards them. I'm thinking this is shaping up nicely. Maybe a big story for this little town and I've got a bead on some great pictures. The police shout instructions to move off the street through a loud-hailer. And that's when the protesters all sit down on the road and keep chanting. Some of them link arms. And they make a pathetic little group really, sitting there with the rain bucketing down. But maybe I can get some closeups of faces and I'm ready for when the police make a move.

There're more police than seems strictly necessary. The protesters go limp and refuse to move. And for every one of them there's two police, and they're big country boys on the whole. Two policemen grab the woman's arms and I'm all ready and primed for some fisticuffs, a bit of hair pulling, a bit of boot sinking, like they've been doing down south. But these big boys pull her up and walk her between them towards the police van. They keep asking her if she's going to obey the police directive. She doesn't say anything. She's stopped chanting. She just stands there, looking a bit angsty but quiet, waits in line with the others at the back of the van.

A policewoman asks her name and writes it on a form. This officer doesn't look like a local. We don't have any women on the squad up here that I know of, and I'm on the court beat most days. I'm in position and get a good shot but it's a bit of an anti-climax really. And then one of the lads in uniform who's been waiting with her gives her a hand up into the back of the van.

Events occurring III

Police officer attending: thoughts

I watch the protesters walk with hands in the air, with all eleven
of them chanting 'The Right to March, The Right to March'.
They're just a small, raggy bunch, hippy looking: all faded shirts,
loose sandals or rubber thongs and torn jeans. They don't seem to
be belligerent or aggressive. Don't seem to be all that confident,
actually. As they come up to the intersection our senior sergeant
tells us to form a line and walk towards them to corral them
against the other line moving in from behind. Shouldn't be hard.
There are more of us than them.

As I get close up, I can see their straining faces, their mouths
moving, but I've zoned out at that point, can't hear what they're
saying. I don't want to mess this up. Maybe they have a point.
They weren't causing anyone any trouble, just the cars had to
edge around them in the narrow street. From the corner of
my eye, I can see my mates in the line, bulky, walking heavily
forward. Boots sticking in the melting bitumen. Blue shirts soggy
in the rain, hat brims dripping down their backs. Senior sergeant
shouts instructions through his loud-hailer at the pitiful little
demo, tells them to move off the street

We surround them as they all sit down on the road and they're still
chanting, chanting. And a couple of them have linked arms.

We work in pairs, like we were told, one on each side. Grab the
woman's arms. Pull her up so she's on her feet. Walk her quick
march towards the police van. I keep asking her if she is going to
obey the police directive, disperse, clear the roadway.

She doesn't say anything. She stops chanting. Catches her breath.
She stands between us in line without a struggle, and we wait at
the back of the van. Then she's being processed.

A policewoman is asking her name and writing it on a form. This is a uniformed officer from the city but I'm sure she's Special Branch, up here to report back to Brisbane Headquarters on the unrest and commie mobs. A photographer from the *The Townsville Bulletin* sneaks in behind us and takes the woman's photo. And then we give her a boost into the back of the van.

Statement to the Magistrate
(source personal files)

illegal street march
disobeying police direction
                    pleaded guilty
                    I do not break laws lightly
                    I was there for a reason
                    it was important
                    to voice my dissent to our government
no power, no wealth, no influence—
the street is our only forum
caring for our democratic liberty
is a matter of conscience
one month to pay
or one month in jail

NOTICE TO A PERSON ADMITTED TO BAIL BY A POLICE OFFICER BY DEPOSIT OF MONEY

That on the 8th day of July 1978, at Townsville in the Magistrates Court District of Townsville in the State of Queensland, one [name of offender] disobeyed a direction given by a member of the Police Force namely [name of arresting officer] in the exercise of his powers under the Traffic Act.

Extract from Form 17C

Notice to a person

in the State of Queensland
in the State of Queensland
in the State of Queensland

ratbag homosexuals
ratbag homosexuals
ratbag homosexuals

disobeyed police direction
disobeyed police direction
disobeyed police direction

member of Police Force
member of Police Force
member of Police Force

exercised his powers
exercised his powers
exercised his powers

judicial use of Traffic Act
judicial use of Traffic Act
judicial use of Traffic Act

communists arrested
dissidents arrested
subversives arrested

NAZI POWERS FOR THE POLICE

The Townsville Daily Bulletin, 1979

Part 3: Surveillance and violence

After the Right to March demonstrations in Brisbane and regional centres such as Townsville, the government handed the police and enforcement agencies new powers to enable them to control citizens and repress dissent. Part of this control was the collating of official files on anyone who came to the notice of authorities for anything deemed anti-social.

Police state blues

Police state blues are scaring us
Gun law propositions for search
without warrant terrifies us

Police could
        Break a person's door down
        Smash in walls, floors, ceilings
        Break open cupboards
        Cast books and clothing all over the floor
                        pretend to look for guns

the twenty percent, they're the worry
police here are known for their corruption

IF IT MEANS SHOOTING PEOPLE ON THE SPOT, IT IS EXCUSABLE

'special surveillance'

The National Times, 1981

Of the 265 incidents of political violence recorded in Australia from 1963 to 1981 only 12 were in Queensland, and five of these were window smashings.

… the Minister for Employment and Labour Relations said:

- 'if people show anti-social behaviour they should be checked out. Police should be given a free hand. If it means shooting people on the spot, it is excusable'.

- '… happy that files were kept on a wide range of people' … 'they did not have to be obviously subversive to have files kept on them'.

- '… assured Queenslanders that they 'have nothing to fear'.

If it means shooting people on the spot, it is excusable

Some words can separate you from your body. And from the world you thought you knew. When you cut the article from the tropical damp newspaper, kitchen scissors not quite steady, your mind won't let these words go. You know it's personal. You know they mean you.

They know you by your body, the unfeminine body of you, in the massing of a protest rally, whether it's twelve people or twelve hundred. Checked shirts, jeans, Doc Martens, smoking roll-your-owns, your body both outraged and an outrage, solid on the melting bitumen street, fists clenched so tight the white skin breaks under your nails, the chanting loud, rhythmic *Close Pine Gap, We Have the Right to March, Gay Pride,* the slogans on the placards bleeding in the rain.

**

They will know you by your mind, the questions, the dissent, the contradictions uncovered, the refusal of the orthodoxy that makes you hot and cold at their careless disregard for your civil liberties. And they will know you from their records, the files they keep, your obviously subversive body and your dangerously subversive mind.

You are one of the Queenslanders who have 'something to fear'. You know their files have words about you. And photos construed as evidence of the dangerously anti-social. Their *Special Surveillance* is directed at you. The dark-suited men taking photos at the entrance to the CAMP club on George Street. The note-taker outside the Lesbian-Feminist Collective meetings. The stranger asking questions that are too personal, too soon, to be a comfortable coincidence.

**

This failure of trust goes both ways. Irreparable, it separates you for the rest of your life. From those who say, 'we just want you to be happy', from the ones who want to be bystanders, and those who counsel 'just try to fit in', 'don't take everything so personally', 'smile more, it makes you look more feminine'.

There can be humour, too, in the failure of trust. The dark sardonic, bitter shiver of danger, the 'what's the worst they can do to me, kill me?' backhander you share with the other *communists, obscene parasites, lunatic fringe, known radicals.*

being one too law-abiding to smash windows
being free with spray can and ready-made slogan politics
there is a line—
my body is on the line
at risk and on file

Part 4: Space for the L Word

Following the Queensland wide civic unrest in response to the street march/demonstration ban, Sydney's first Gay Mardi Gras on June 24th 1978, catapulted from a fun event to brutal, systematic bashings and arrests by police. We followed the happenings from our rural and small-town vantage point in the far north, appalled at the viciousness and gratuitous violence of the police.

The other memorable thing for us in Mardi Gras (apart from the interest of the police), was the *Dykes on Bikes* contingent. From Townsville we could only look on with pride and envy. Their bikes were all at least 750cc road bikes, some of them bigger, and packing grunt that we had no hope of managing, some of them Harleys. Although we had pretensions to bikie identity, in reality, I was a pale scaredy-cat and failed at 'Being Tough 101', with no tattoos and a yellow jacket with my name inked on the label in the lining.

Following on from the first Gay Mardi Gras, we saw a blossoming of Gay and Lesbian Conferences, Women's Festivals, Lesbian Feminist activities, all of which promoted an awakening pride in identity, academic explorations and theorising of gendered consciousness.

enemy of the State

my history was taken
by a break
and enter …
stolen

a trinket box   (jewels are too grandiose description
                    although the memories left as residue
                    from protest and dissent,
                    are gold and silver now)

thieved in malice—

                    along with the Bronze Medallion and
                    Bar, Argonauts badge (Segesta 6) and

Rainbow Pride
Sexism puts down half the world
Sexism is men's feet on women's necks
Gay Pride
I AM AN ENEMY OF THE STATE
You can't sink a rainbow (Rainbow Warrior)
Peace
Hiroshima Never again
Woman's Place is in the House and in the Senate
No uranium
Silence is the offence

What was left?
        a **Fuck Housework** badge

a solitary standout (looking not important)
gold letters on maroon, oval shaped
the traditional Australian battle arena
discreetly pinned on a forty-year-old
pea coat

and a single earring, a Minoan double axe which only ever
accompanies female goddesses

YEAR OF THE LESBIAN

The Australian, 1983

YEAR OF THE NON- EXISTENT

The Courier Mail, 1983

Space for the L word: a brief history of second wave feminism (where claiming a liberty is rarely civil) and the resultant horrification of the conservative community when the deviants escape from the constraints of discourse.

We are a society of separations, divisions, schisms, burnt bridges and steps too far. In 1983 men, women, feminists, gays and lesbians use the rhetorics of extremism to cement our points of disagreement, absolutist difference and outrageous repression of rights, claims of liberties of expression and association.

The leader of the National Party (beige safari suits, comb-over rather than mullet) says the Party's wives (cardigans and pearls) believe the government's sex discrimination legislation is a 'crusade by feminists' motivated by their 'hatred of men', and disdain for the 'women who want to be women' who prefer to be 'home-makers' (cardigans, pearls *and* aprons).

These men and 'their' women speak of the Women's Liberation Movement as if they are holding some badly smelling words gingerly with their fingertips to remove the odour to another place and time where it has no impact on their thought processes.

So, when the feminists (unwashed, unkempt Women's Land women) then articulate discomfort with including lesbians (overalls, unshaven legs and armpits, big boots, big hair or shaved head man-haters) in the movement in case the lesbians give them a bad name, we move from the closet to the articulation of gay rights and gay power, and the feminists call it a negative, hostile reaction.

We come to a decision point then, the question of the decade (it is, after all, the 80s): do we align our politics with straight women or with gay men (neither group in open arms welcome)?

And with this tenuous, debatable, alignment split constantly fracturing, there is a firing up of mutual resentment and antagonism between, within and around every nominal gender group at the first sign of stress.

However, we (the Ls of the LGBTIQ) triumph (white horse/knight/shining/positively glittering armour). Galloping over the horizon, heroic thundering to our salvation, giving space to our inclusion needs, comes a place in the rainbow alphabet. The letters roll off the tongue, (no uncomfort, upset or discomposure), LGBTQIAAA+ (the plus sign added to circumvent/pre-empt any possible group being excluded to the cold outer of the gender discourse wars). So, we're in if we're out, but only in moderation, in all senses of the sentence.

And that is the saga of the discomforting of the discourse when it was opened to the possibilities and contradictions of the coming out story of gender.

The many years of the Lesbian I

We called it the 'Year of the Lesbian', a bit tongue-in-cheek, but not completely. We wanted to get out and visible, a bit blatant, an in-your-face statement of existential intent. And we were not completely unprepared for the backlash when the Australian Union of Students declared 1983 the International Year of the Lesbian, but the outcry still came with a stomach roiling apprehension. It was all in the papers, a bit of excitement as the social unease with our aberrance did its own coming out.

It's the last straw headlined *The Australian... far too extreme... These people are almost jumping off the edge of the earth when it comes to extremism.* And a strange call, even then, the *Year of the Non-existent* in the *Courier Mail*, referring to Queen Victoria's understanding that lesbians don't exist, and the commentator's opinion that it is a shame that isn't the way it is still.

They tried to make us disappear then, to ignore us, castigate us and cover us with sarcasm and opprobrium. Now, nearly forty years on, vaccinated voluntarily, eagerly and to the full, with all the intervening years being Lesbian Years, I'm still here. Even though I'm one of the 'almost dead', trumping Trump's disregard with my longevity, I'm still here. Now forgetting that forty years ago they wanted us gone, at this moment our aged bodies are useful, lesbian or not, to test the vaccine that was developed with desperate haste. Oh, the irony is not lost on the lesbian. Now our aged, lesbian bodies, incarcerated in aged care facilities, high risk and vulnerable, have a use-value.

The many years of the Lesbian II

Sign here they said, *if you can't manage your signature, due to your advanced age, just make your mark, X marks the spot.* And, if I do sign, am I more likely to get the virus, die, or in some other way have a bad experience? Apparently, it would be worse than a bad case of daydreaming and may have a precipitous ending. And my dreaming of past heartfelt, heartrending, love heart events, Year of the Lesbian events... who is to say this past dreaming is worse than the heart was at the time? *Put your finger on it*, they said, *the X...take some risks for us...make yourself useful, reduce the care burden the elderly put on the rest of us.*

During my doonah sleep-in, daydreaming, best-time-of-the-day times, I need to be extra careful now that my *niksen* times (delicious Dutch word meaning 'doing nothing') are not mistaken for my time-of-death-time.

The many years of the Lesbian III

On the day of the millionth case and half million deaths I drink coffee in a warm morning living room, walk a small dog at our national Arboretum, eat a lesbian lunch of seafood and avocado at a local outdoor café, buy two likely looking lesbian books on Amazon, tune into a Zoom poetry reading and listen to podcasts from america.

Realise it's the end of the world, as we know it. Noting that while the *Year of the Non-Existent* didn't catch on, COVID-19 has caught on, and may well be the death of us. On this evening, as the dark of 2020's longest night seeps in, I peel a bright, loose skinned mandarin, the pith and tart of the skin causing a poodle to sneeze.

Sweet, sweet juice in my mouth flooding, flooding…

WOMEN MAY TRY TO ENTER PINE GAP

The Canberra Times, 1983

Women Make a Peace Banner

The National Times, 1983

Part 5: We join the rest of the country

We join the rest of the country in a nationally planned women's movement peace protest, heady days for girls from FNQ Mango Collective. For the first time we feel we are really radically activist in a national sense. Groups of women from all over the country organise ourselves into small, local, mutually supportive collectives, give ourselves less than important names and sew identity banners so we can find each other at the camp. We head off to Alice Springs and the gates of the Pine Gap US satellite surveillance base known at the time as the Joint Defence Space Research Facility run by the CIA.

I went from Townsville to Mt Isa and Alice Springs by bus and alighted in the unwelcoming local street to find my sleeping bag had been stolen somewhere between when the driver threw our gear onto the footpath and when I managed to shoulder my way through the onlookers to pick up my backpack. In town, the pub and local shops would not serve us, and waiting staff in cafes pretended we were not there.

HUMAN RIGHTS COMMISSION

REPORT NO. 20 COMPLAINTS RELATING TO THE PROTEST
AT PINE GAP, NOVEMBER 1983–OCTOBER 1986

Australian Government Publishing Service, Canberra 1986.

Chapter 1 The Inquiry

Arising out of the demonstration at Pine Gap in the Northern Territory
in November 1983 by Women for Survival, the Commission received thirty-
nine complaints of infringements of human rights…

12. The main issues raised with the AFP, along with a reference to the
relevant human rights in the International Covenant on Civil and Political
Rights (ICCPR) (text at Appendix 5), were:

> the use of the AFP helicopter during the protest (Articles 21 and
> 22.1)
> the way in which protesters were selected for arrest (Article 9.1)
> delays in informing the complainants of the charges against them
> (Article 9.2)

In relation to the Northern Territory Police Force, the main matters, again
with a reference to the relevant ICCPR Articles (text at Appendix 5),
were:

> the manner in which fingerprints were obtained (Articles 7 and
> 10.1)
> the strip searching of complainants (Articles 10.1, 7 and 17)
> access to legal advice (Article 14(3)(b)) access to medical
> attention (Articles 10 and 7)
> general atmosphere and attitudes (Articles 3, 7, 10.1, 14.3(a) and (b)
> and 26)

Pine Gap I

Overheard in End of the Road Bar, *any Friday night, Alice Springs, 1983*

We've been dazzled by the mumbo-jumbo. Pine Gap is about espionage, the biggest spy game you can think of. It's in the heart of our country and it's not even ours. It's the Americans, their own private spy base. They're using satellites to listen in on a huge range of communications and other electronic signals.

What makes us, or anyone really, think that it won't be used for aggression?

Pine Gap II

Mango Collective Member

The night is cooling off quickly as we start to shiver in our day-time thin cotton shirts and hiking shorts designed for 40 degrees Celsius. We're from Mango country around Townsville and Cairns so we weren't really expecting these freezing nights. We zip up our jackets and scuffle around in the tent looking for beanies and socks. The stars are coming out and the moon is not yet up. We walk along the fence looking for a spot to get over but that's not going to work, so back at the gate we wait. There is some sort of commotion up near the edge of the camp on the road and we think it's the Alice Springs lout mobs in their dickhead utes come to harass us again.

But tonight, the ruckus is good for us, so we slip around the barrier post and run like the dickens into the dark low scrub. Shit! We're actually inside the base now. Seven years in jail if we're caught! In-camera hearing and evidence destroyed. Crikey! We could just be disappeared! But this is Australia, right! Right! And, if we're arrested out here at Pine Gap, we are told to all give our names as *Karen Silkwood*. Anyway, we're still running, up a small scrubby rise and further into the desert dark. And we're hoping like hell the helicopters with spotlights are not coming over until we've been and gone. When we stop, we're looking for a place to leave the Mango Collective banner. We want it to be seen. It's a beautiful thing and we're torn about not taking it home with us. It's to let them know we did the illegal entry. But it's tricky in the dark to find a place. It'll look quite different when the sun comes up. In the end, we wedge the banner into a couple of low branches on a scrubby bush and hope they'll find it.

Later, back in the grubby sleeping bags, the adrenalin ebbs a bit, we stop the hysterical recounting, the breathing settles down. We add this one to our 'actions', try to weight down the tent edges so the hovering helicopters don't send our tent off after the banner or out into the desert.

Pine Gap III

At the gate

We were a non-violent protest but that didn't mean we were passive. When the massed protesters that day did a mock play on how to jump over the gate we laughed and then the mob of us surged against the gate. It was an ordinary metal stock gate with two bolts to hold it closed against a post, and metal hinges. The gate was the point of the protest. The gate was what closed the road to us, the demonstrators, and to the general Australian public.

The gate opened by the police every shift change as the workers from inside the base were bussed out and a new bus came in. And they were your big white 56-seaters. When they roared down the narrow road with our tents and swags and so on all down the edges it was a miracle they didn't run over someone. They were scared I think that there would be some sort of action against them if they slowed down too much, but it was really dangerous for us.

Anyway, when the surge of bodies happened, the gate bent. We lifted it off its hinges and carried it out of the mass to the side. It was gone in minutes. Bits of wire, metal pipes, the hinges, the bolts all magicked into nothing.

The police came through later asking about whether we knew anything about where the gate was, we smirked and said no. And we took all the little bits of that gate home with us, far and wide, all across Australia.

Pine Gap IV

Helicopter pilot

Yeah, we were deployed most nights of the camp to fly over and put the fear of God into them. It was harassment. Nothing to hurt them. They didn't know that. If we got low enough the wind surge of sand and dust would catch a few tents and fill their sleeping bags with grit and so on. We were told to use the spotlight on any of them near the fence, especially the gate. They kind of dared themselves to do the illegal entry, I think, so there were always some to pick out in the light. It was nothing personal, but I mean, what kind of woman would go out there to behave like that. They had it coming... well, whatever was coming, I guess. I mean, they deserved all they got. And some of the town hoons used to go out there to scare the shit out of them and rough them up a bit. One ute drove through a few tents. One time the yokels actually grabbed two women and put them in the back of a ute, then dumped them back on the road to town. No harm done, just the lads being a bit excessive. The police were always out there though, so that put the dampeners on anything too much over the line. None of us did anything like that, but. You know, the uniform and so on, and we had our orders. We just did the noise and spotlights and stirring up the sand.

Pine Gap V

The police officer who cried

They weren't all against us. I know that. They were just doing their jobs. But when we stood face-to-face along the police phalanx and we sang to them, *We are gentle, angry women and we're singing, singing for our lives* some of the women in uniform looked away, couldn't look at us. And one of the women cried.

POOFS IN THE PARK

The Townsville Advertiser, 1980

BEWARE THE GAY INVADERS

The Townsville Advertiser, 1984

Homosexual teachers out

The Courier Mail, 1983

Part 6: Will they ever let us work?

The public discourse of the north and of the times was illuminating and frightening. A young gay teacher who had graduated from his course was not given a teaching post because he was a leading activist in the campaign to allow gay and lesbian teachers to be employed by the Department of Education. Teacher trainees at this point were bonded by the Department to teach for two years anywhere they were posted in the State to repay the cost of their training. It was unheard of to be not posted if the course was successfully completed. The outrage from everywhere was palpable. But it was outrage that there were gay and lesbian teachers actually teaching in Queensland schools. We believed that there were so many of us that if we were all sacked the school system would fall in on itself. The Far North Queensland community outdid itself in blazing words across the headlines that characterised us as outsiders who took our careers in our hands if we came out or were even suspected of being 'deviant'.

Concatenation Conversation Education 1983

Gay academic: There could be as many as 10,000 homosexuals living in Townsville, we're a city of 10,000 gays

Local politician: Homosexuality is 'unnatural' and condemned by all major religions. We should beware the Gay Invaders

Mother of two: I agree. Homosexuality is perversion, repulsive and sordid. It's not just a case of two men holding hands. I know of a young man who *They* converted to homosexuality

Former nursing sister: It's a known fact that people involved as homosexuals for any lengthy period end up with a rare form of schizophrenia

Mother of two: The stress of discovering a homosexual in a family is enormous. In one family with two heterosexual sons, a third was homosexual and this caused the father to have a nervous breakdown. It's in the newspaper

Letter to the editor: Primary school children, it would seem, are to be assisted towards homosexuality

Local politician: They're all ideological fanatics, lesbians, homosexuals, and of course communists (of both the Moscow and Peking variety) and left wingers of all sorts…

Gay academic: And there they go, off on a little queer bashing

Journalist: It's great copy, Poofs in the Park, wandering homosexuals

Education Minister: They're not getting any leave to attend the Australian Teachers' Federation Melbourne Conference on homosexual and lesbian teachers. We don't employ them, homosexuals I mean. I'm having research done to discover the extent of them in the department

Regional Director of Education, Northern Region: Homosexual Teachers are out. They're repugnant to the decent, average Australian. Such teachers would be deviates

MLA Queensland: Openly gay teachers in schools are one thing. The Education Department continues to employ thousands of silent homosexuals and lesbians in its schools

Local solicitor: We should ask some experts in the fields of education, sociology, psychology and psychiatry, acknowledged experts in their general fields whether there are any reasons for supposing that a self-avowed homosexual is not a fit and proper person to teach children in a primary school, because they're being singled out for this especially vicious treatment. These attacks don't seem right

Silent lesbian: [   ]

Self-avowed homosexual: Crikey!

LETTER OF REPLY

At times, during the decade of protest my disenchantment with the government grew unbearable. My sense of forcible rejection and alienation were palpable. At one point a group of us individually wrote to the Prime Minister offering a donation to promote world peace. We thought a financial contribution would indicate our valuing of such a concept.

At the same time, we felt really special (sardonically), because we lived in Queensland and were surveilled, recorded, watched, reported on, filed and generally named as 'persons of interest'.

I am returning your contribution

In the file: Letter of reply from Prime Minister, Canberra, 29 March 1982

Thank you for your correspondence
with which you enclosed a donation to the cause
of world peace.
There is, however, no Government body or agency
which is legally or administratively designed
to accept your contribution…

I am returning your contribution…

not deviant?

The Weekend Australian Magazine, 1985

If you live in Queensland…

If you live in Queensland…
Beware
You are being watched
Your strange activities or preferences will be noted
The Minister for Justice (irony duly noted) has introduced
amendments to the Liquor Bill
If you are a:

- Drug dealer
- Sexual pervert
- Deviant
- Child molester

you are banned from drinking in Queensland bars
Licensees are sufficiently worldly to identify these people

Dare we say it… the Legislation is a poofter-bashing witch-hunt
aimed at the gay community, a crack-down on undesirables…

If you are an undesirable…
If you live in Queensland…
Beware
You are being watched

radio news is disappointing

She pulls on her swimming shorts. The air is cold, deadly, soul
destroying, like public opinion, seeping slow and unpleasant into the
pool change room.

> who knows what to think…
> cognitive capture
> is a thing — mind-fog, non-logic

Radio news goes on and on, shouting off the cement walls, words
running amok, numbers so big they're meaningless. Big stories of the
day are election pouting, celebrity outing. China, Ukraine, COVID,
flu and off-line power generators. The excessive numbers shroud any
vivid futures.

She shrugs into a towelling robe, uneasy, living the moment, being
her best self, hostage to what she doesn't know, outcomes of public
opinion, radio call-in and shock-jocks. Her body is policed and all she
wants to do is swim.

> which bodies can swim?
> whose 'comfortable satisfaction'
> is she up against?

Part 7: Now, who is left standing?

Fast forward to the first Brisbane Pride Festival in 1990. And hopefully, the weight of the social is more inclusive. More generous. More gender flexible. Grown up and mature. But no. Featured in the news is the protester with his sign 'grotty perverts and poofters, you're parasites. Sick people'. This is why our rage grows.

This is why, when the Gay Pride street march in Brisbane moved on to the Victoria Bridge and a man drove an old ute into the marchers, someone jumped onto the car bonnet to stop him. And, terrifically thrilling, this is why a woman kicked in his headlights.

These outrages of separation I felt are not unique to either me or the times. Gay men and lesbians have sociologically been border people for many years and, even now, forty years on from my decade of unease, can be made borderline again without notice. From the misappropriation of First Nations land by invading settlers, through gender diverse, flexible androgyny found in articles found from 1863, 1956, 1967, 1983, and 1998 I find intersectional issues in a long history of misogyny stretching to the present-day opprobrium and vilification.

Now, after these unrested decades, it is fair to ask who is left standing? What has changed and what is the legacy? The answer is less than promising as we move on through the 90s and 2000s with the weight of a century of oppression, homophobia and misogyny still lifted each morning, thrown into the air and carried through every day.

Transport Canberra Lost Property report

'When claiming a lost item, you must be the owner of the item…You may be required to provide evidence that you are the owner of the item, such as proof of purchase or a description of the item.'

Form reference code 85DFQ2

Ticket to ride: Whose country?

For you it starts with a ticket to ride the bus. This proves you are not impecunious, itinerant, stony broke or on your uppers. Indeed, the ticket proves you have an acceptable place to go, that you have something to lose.

And then you lose it…an item, the item, your item. It could be your glasses (because you can read, after all), or your pen (ditto writing). Or your left behind girlfriend (because ownership of the person is definitely an issue).

**

Or your briefcase, lost, and in it, evidence of privilege, (your privilege) and unlawful residence (this country on which the bus is driving has never been ceded, given over, given up). Documentary evidence of ownership of land to which you are not entitled, taken by invasion. Documents you believe are proof of purchase, your ownership.

And when you describe your lost item, that stuffed briefcase, try to describe the Country, describe with felicity the previous custodians of the country, because that knowledge is not written in the evidentiary reports contained in your lost briefcase.

**

When you lodge your Lost Property Report *Please be aware that not all items that are reported lost are located.*

You may claim and claim, but you came late. You cannot prove the Country knows you or recognises you. The briefcase you need is lost.

The documents are gone. You have nothing, not even the Country you are standing on.

FOUND DEAD IN WOMEN'S CLOTHES

Central Queensland Herald, 1956

Dead women's clothes

FOUND **DEAD**
IN **WOMEN'S**
CLOTHES
SYDNEY,October15. –
Detectives are **baffled at**
the death of an ███████ **inspector**
found **hanged** and
wearing women's clothing at
███ Sydney.
The man, █████████████
████, █████████████
Sydney, was **married** and the
father of two children, aged
13 and12. He was **found** in
the home of a relative.
Friends said today they
could not understand why he
should be wearing women's
clothing and that **they had**
never been given any **indication**
that **he was** anything but
normal.

████████████████
████████████████
████████

The body was **dressed** in a
woman's blouse,
corsets,
women's shoes,

stockings,
brassiere
and other female
attire

He was last seen alive on
Friday night, when he left
home saying that he was going

to a meeting to arrange a
███████ Christmas party.

I

THE **MAN IN WOMAN**'S CLOTHES.
TO THE **EDIT**OR OF THE ARGUS

Sir,-**I was the man** employed at the Poly
technic Institution, who **detected** the man
███████████ who **dressed in woman's clothes**
in Collingwood. I have been since discharged
from my situation, because my employer says
I got a **free o**rder for the admission of a
woman of bad character into the Institute.
But the reason I got the free order, without
telling anyone, was because if I told anyone
I should not have caught **the person I was**
after. Besides, I knew the woman **would
look respectable,** or she would **not** have been
admitted. Will you kindly publish this, to
clear my character? It is because the **case
was so bad** that you would **no**t publish the
evidence that **all this has** not **come out.**
Yours obediently.

███████████████

II

THE MAN IN **WOMAN'S CLOTHES**.
TO THE EDITOR OF THE ARGUS

Sir, **I was the man** employed at the Poly
technic Institution, **who detected the man**
██████████ who **dressed in woman's clothes**
in Collingwood. **I have been** since **discharged**
from my situation, because my employer says
I got a free order for the admission of a
wo**man of bad character** into the Institute.
But the reason I got the free order, **without**
telling anyone was because if I told anyone
I should not have **caught** the person I was
after. Besides, I knew the woman would
look respectable, or she would not have been
admitted. Will you kindly publish this, **to**
clear my character? It is because the case
was so bad that you would not publish the
evidence that **all this has not come out**.
Yours obediently,

██████████████

gossip columnist unmasked
as out of time

outing is a power play, gossip of the worst sort
so far from best interests
or public interest, beneath any radar of who cares
designed to take down, beat up
a rebel flouting rules of convention on
gender expectation — outing is voyeuristic observation

no journalist, just a prurient gossip columnist
thinking of a scoop revelatory
of celebrity sexuality

no-one deserves their cover blown
but wait, bird's flown,
she's taken back her narrative
from newspaper hijacking,
editorial is pouting, true, story had an outing
but too late, all over bar the shouting

Dressing the part

The Bulletin, 1967

dressing the part girls

skid affairs girls girls trying to go straight good
and their scarves signified satin those a-wings loose
girls stayed with organdie and worn decently
are all dead who again dress to entertain (was the abandoned Don?)

like a lamp-post with organdie was dots ... the regular stars are dots
bad berets, something to polka, it's Faye and off-the-shoulder curls
on her neck telling polka-dot blouses as ambiguous big show off Ameche
made Alice domestic. Alice, black, aglow, Westerns are OK.

a cloudy blouse worn morally by the heroine, she'd one time black net.
Claire has polka, just and different to Betty Grable. Broad skirt, hair from
honkytonks glued-down. Trevor the intruder sins, he meant apron
buttoned,
common is stockings, transition to marriage bound, tasteful and shows
singing.

your better-type diamond cotton makes bliss

star clothes long to be foreign. Hepburn is inconclusive. It came from the
stars
It's symbolic, become else, supposes there's clothes end.
Most and very covering, if co-stars like busts and waists. like Russell
worn by likely things circa all English. It didn't end in cleavage,

as when spend naked, she's a big sad, to have even the all,
films, days apparel, these confusing to whom it's a matter of Balenciaga,
of wriggling Jane eyes, of the end, the film (much with captions)...
the Givenchy or she the Audrey ... what one sheet of cloth problem!

Beer poured on Romeo

London –
A girl who was sacked after tipping beer
over an office Romeo has won
the first tribunal-heard sexual harassment case
under the Sex Discrimination Act.

The Townsville Daily Bulletin, 1983

I

Beer and breasts don't mix
Poured half a pint, over him, office Romeo, wasted on him,
On all his mates, who think the party is for them,
        a hunting party
Office girl is fair game, they're after breasts and
        neck, and thighs without consent
Romeo in action, grabbing, prodding, touching, skin
        crawls under unwanted hands
Hurt doesn't cut it, not really, it's assault in action,
        full view. Five hundred dollars for
'Feelings'! Understatement, creeping hands need scrubbing
        off, gag-reflex

II

it's still 1983 in the Far North
or anywhere in the Antipodes, really—
a bar is a bar is a bar
avoidance posture for any girl who wants a drink
no protection in the Ladies Lounge
alcohol and men and sexual predation combination
makes us act with excruciating trepidation
around any watering hole
beer is assault is rape is cover-up
you should have covered-up
beer and breasts don't mix

DYKES BASHED, NO ARRESTS

Lesbians on the Loose, 1998

Rikki and Del, and their friends Zugs and Myrtle, go out for a quiet drink at a pub on Saturday night

It is 1998

A *horrific bashing* in a Sydney pub put three women in hospital with serious injuries

andyetnotoneofthetenmenwhotookpartintheviolencehasbeenarrested.

nowitnessescameforward

Rikki, her girlfriend Del and their friend Zugs were walking along Balmain Road after a Saturday night out at the Leichhardt Hotel

And as they came to the Bald-Faced Stag Hotel they decided to nip in for a last one before going home (as one does).

Ayoungmanstandingonthefootpath,*allegedly*hitDelintheface,*kickedher*-tookherwatch.

Zugs told the man they didn't want any trouble,

Delwas**hit**ontheheadwithapoolcueand***kickedbythreemen.***

Zugs went to her rescue.   Shewas*attacked*and***kickedtotheground.***

nowitnessescameforward

Themen'sgirllfriendseggingthemon,screaming,

'bashem,they'renothingbutdykes!'

*10men*wereattackingthewomenusingpoolcuesand*theirboots.*

Othermenjoinedin—

nowitnessescameforward

Rikki: fractured skull and cheekbone, ruptured stomach and torn bowel…

Doctors are hoping that as the blood on her brain dissolves, her hearing will return.

Del and Zugs spent time in hospital recovering from their wounds. Thebarstaff *'didnothing'*topreventtheviolence

police*eventually*arrivedtherewerenoarrestsas*nowitnessescameforward.*

Detectives now say there is an *attempted murder investigation.*

Good friend Myrtle says it was a *hate crime,* deliberate, a night of *dyke bashing…*

Nowitnessescameforward

Part 8: Opprobrium, still…

Visit Queensland: Home of the BIGs

The Big Apple, Stanthorpe The Big Banana, North Mackay The Big Barramundi, Normanton The Big Barramundi, Daintree The Big Brolga, Townsville The Big Bottle, Bundaberg The Big Bull, Rockhampton The Big Cane Toad, Sarina The Big Captain Cook, Cairns The Big Cassowary, Mission Beach The Big Cow, Nambour The Big Crab, Cardwell The Big Crab, Miriam Vale The Big Crocodile, Daintree The Big Crocodile, Hartley's Creek The Big Crocodile, Normanton The Big Dugong, Rockhampton The Big Dinosaur, Ballandean The Big Easel, Emerald The Big Gumboot, Tully The Big Macadamia Nut, Nambour The Big Mandarin, Mundubbera The Big Mango, Bowen The Big Marlin, Cairns The Big Hard Rock Guitar, Surfers Paradise The Big Merino, Blackall

Why am I making a BIG Thing about the BIGs? Because Queensland is about BIG. What they do in Queensland is usually BIG, out of proportion, over the top.

Coming back to the 80s from 2021 what the discourse allowed seems outrageous from our new sensibilities of inclusion and appropriateness.

The Big mumbo-jumbo, The Big con, The Big misogynist homophobic hatred, The Big gay and lesbian bashing decades, The Big discrimination against gay teachers, The Big fear of strong, LOUD women, The Big repression of peace activists, The Big fear of civic protest, The Big legislated racial discrimination policies, The Big…(fill in the gaps)

What the discourses of the 80s that are still turning up in 2021 show us is the fragility of the gains we thought we had made against misogyny, homophobia, repressions of freedoms.

Remember, the past is alive in us, all the time. We move through and against our history, reference our own creation stories, time and time again, to our own unique experience of past events. We are separated, enraged. The opprobrium of the continuing present will not allow us moderation. Or allow us to forgive. Nor mellow. Nor soften. Nor excuse. We will not forget, condone, pardon what was done to us in the name of normative heterogeneity.

We are the unforgiving...

'Drunks, Homosexuals, Adulterers, Liars, Fornicators, Thieves, Atheists, Idolators: Hell Awaits You'

Israel Folau, 2019

Freedoms

It has not been like this, always,
dividing gays and straights with walls
of ferocious argument that makes no sense, because
you're never clear from whom you're desperate to protect
yourselves—from preening queens or diesel dykes? Sometimes
it's just a fantasy of difference, theology, that puts us on the outside.

Man-made separations, imagined threat to you and yours, force us to the outside
and now with trans and queer, you double-down, a man's a man, always!
Not being clear on inter-sex or trans, or gay, or lesbian, sometimes,
you literally bash a poofter, leave them bloody, against a wall.
We don't go out these days, fear the fists, spit and slagging off, we protect
ourselves from you, your rage and your religion, because

it could be you, I'm ranting at, because
I can't be sure, your voting power gone wild, outside
your usual calm and rational view, buttons pressed, you protect
yourselves from gays and queers and trans, as if we're after you. Always
your straitened gender, as if you're under threat, a dogma wall
to keep us out (or keep us in, it's not clear, sometimes).

When you legislate your right to vilify us, sometimes
the mood music to the times is now, in social media posts, because
linking sexuality and sin are you, your writing, projecting on the wall,
religious quotes that damn us to living on the outside.
Your social order discriminates against us. Always,
your religious freedom sounds like a need to hurt us, *your* speech protect.

Religious freedom, as a right, lets you rant against us. You protect,
provoke the hate crimes, to punish and control, assert your norms. Sometimes,
because you think you have the moral right, you want to save us. Always,
this is hurtful and full of danger, you sending us to your hell, because
with this law you're free to rant against us — on the steps, outside
your church, on any airwaves, twitter, facebook, anywhere outside your wall.

With self-righteous dogma you can preach, evangelise, build a wall
to keep us both outside *and* locked inside our closets, to protect
your social order and your norms. But, starting from the outside—
sick with the diatribe of dog-whistles, trolls, hate crimes — sometimes
the dykes, the gays, queers, inter-sex, a trans or two, *stand-up*, because
our revolution is worth the worst that you can do, always.

Our government and you build hate-speech walls, sometimes
you justify by master's tools, master's house '*Laws protect us all from you,
because*
you're outside our social order, always, always'.

COVID-19 pandemic put a halt to progress toward gender equality

Group Processes & Intergroup Relations, 2021

on imagining Frankenstein

Mary imagines Frankenstein, then she conjures a vision of the Last Man, apocalyptic, dystopian, alone, with the perilous pandemic breathed through lungs and blood. Certainly, a Monster, but *her* monster.

Anastasia, Jacinda and Angela imagine catastrophe in the case numbers, close borders and spell out the ground rules. Have the imagination to put health and lives above money and business. Understand the monster of The Collapse of The Economy.

Sabra Klein imagines, tests, learns from the data that oestrogen allows women to generate a more robust immune system than men. She is vilified by her male scientist colleagues as 'Immuno-feminist'. A new Frankenstein?

A new computer model has no imagination. Only future projections to use societal changes, animal behaviour and the changing environment in a mathematical formula to predict where Ebola might strike next, models the next vulnerability. Is unaware that the outcomes it generates may be skewed by gendered human behaviour.

Behaviour becoming visible under pressure of the pandemic shows up the unequal and gendered relations between men and women in glaring technicolour.

Imagine the normative heterogeneity worrying about whose fault it is that we all turned out gay, or bi, or trans, or ... or ...

Imagine Frankenstein... imagine the monster
Imagine the solution... humanity before money ...
Humanity before repression and oppression of difference...
my difference

'women were being burdened by society's notions of how they should live their lives'

Smithsonian Magazine, 2021

Even so, she dresses up nicely

she's in the bath, in four critical inches of tank water,
washing off
1080 rabbit poison
worming drench
sheep dip
sweat
cow shit
poddy calf drool
saddle dubbin
engine grease
dust turned to mud
ingrained general grime
blood
snot
she attends to
grazed knee
bruised shoulder
rope burns
blackened thumb nail
splinters
wind burn
sun burn
callused palm
barbed wire scratches
rough heels
blackheads
cold sores
split ends
back ache

oily hair
dry hair
dry skin
sunspots
melanoma options

she tidies up
    hair, eyebrows, chin, legs, underarms, fingernails, toenails
she avoids the mirror
    flossing, toothpaste, mouthwash gargle
she adds value
deodorant, hair mousse, moisturiser (hands, heels, face, elbows),
    sunscreen SPF50
she ignores
make-up, perfume, hair spray, nail polish
she dresses
    clean shirt, clean undies, clean socks, clean jeans, clean boots
she attends to detail
    colour co-ordinated hanky, hand-tooled leather belt with trophy
      buckle
she covers up the body
    sheepskin jacket, akubra hat

she's scrubbed up pretty nicely and all tooled up

When women cut their hair

When women cut their hair, it has all become so terrible. Women, whose hands have taken into their own hands their fury, their incandescent rage. Hair sheared off, rough cut, chunks and hanks flung in the faces of the jeering, morality police.

When women cut their hair, men should be afraid. Those men of you, sitting quiet, as if there is no line to cross. We know why you are afraid. We want to know why you will not change it.

When women cut their hair, the social order trembles, disordered. Attempts to bring down the patriarchy remain ongoing...

society was undermining women in order to keep them at home under the moniker 'occupation: housewife'

Smithsonian Magazine, 2021

Things rarely go
without a hitch and
someone should have
checked

Too big
Too small
Too long
Too short
Unwanted gift
Too late
Faulty
Colour not as expected
Quality not as expected
   Not my style

Ordered two sizes
Wrong item sent
Looks different from image
Changed my mind
   Addressee has moved on

a 'firefighting masculinity' that trades on ageism, sexism and homophobia, disputes the worth of women and other types of male firefighters on the fireline

University of Wollongong Magazine, 2007

Not too sad, remembering the menace of a lover in a triolet

fires of the summer are burning up Australia
like my many red-hot lovers
their destructiveness caused by our own behaviour
fires of the summer are burning up Australia
fascinated by their menace, by a pattern not familiar
scorching through the hinterland until euphoria is over
fires of the summer are burning up Australia
like my many red-hot lovers

Bullying and discrimination against LGBTI people

ABC News, 2018

Dykes of the seventies send a message to the 2020s via villanelle

We're lesbians, we're queer, we cause a storm
No need to take a position, an agenda
We're on the edge, we're defiantly the norm

It's not as though we care at all for form
For you, my feelings always verge on tender
We're lesbians, we're queer, we cause a storm

It's not as though our love is lorn
As lesbians we've no trouble with our gender
We're on the edge, we're defiantly the norm

Our finery is not what's normally worn
In jeans and boots we're sometimes the offender
We're lesbians, we're queer, we cause a storm

Your hatred of queers only makes us yawn
We don't need your hate-mail, just return to sender
We're on the edge, we're defiantly the norm

We break the mould, we break the form
The form of us, no masking render
We're lesbians, we're queer, we cause a storm
We're on the edge, we're defiantly the norm

'gender equality …
a long way off …
further undermined
by the pandemic'

António Guterres, 2021

Even more so, a villanelle paean for all dykes

This is a song of girls in the limning
a villanelle paean for all dykes who are hurting
in COVID times, a song still worth singing

what is it we are to the debate bringing?
their own forms against them… master's tools furling!
this is a song of girls in the limning

women with cause, with outrage brimming
cancel culture bonus — misogynists squirming
in COVID times, a song still worth singing

no need or hint for our bright lights dimming
she dresses as 'they', her wardrobe diverging
This is a song of girls in the limning

turn up our spotlight, we're playing at winning
debatable gender, boys and girls merging
in COVID times, a song still worth singing

this song is our song, our freedom giving
we're feminists, dykes, queers — together we're
surging
This is a song of girls in the limning
in COVID times, a song still worth singing

homosexuality ... removed from the World Health Organisation's International Classification of Diseases

The Canberra Times, 1990

chemical brain-flood of oxytocin

It's been a pretty ordinary sort of year so far (that is, a year in the not-so-good range), probably most people would agree. So, when the neurochemical, oxytocin, over-ran her brain, she suddenly found an unfamiliar urge to social bonding, found the whole world population to be her family, clan, a racial kinship, and not merely the common DNA originating in the Garden of Eden. She felt a pithy over-wroughtness of religious aphorism—generosity is the antidote to greed, giving is better than receiving, do unto others etc—of no discernible benefit to the wronged or starved.

On a scale commensurate with her Aunt's admonition that 'diamonds are a girl's best friend', she felt selflessly magnanimous, but bereft at lacking her own personal benefactor in either a government pension or invitation to a philanthropic soirée to raise funds for hydroxychloroquine and personal protective equipment.

Holding out her hands, empty, palms up in peace, giving all the skin she has, she realises that a largesse of forgiveness and generalised kindness is not enough. Without the tempered steel of rage and dissent, no-one will move over to make room for her. And she will need more than a chemical brain-flood of oxytocin to move over for anyone else.

Nationally 38.4 per cent voted 'no', representing 4.9 million people

The Canberra Times, 2017

beef city and the lesbian

I go out into the regions away from this cat-filled city,
places I know where they eat more beef! they're back-block battlers,
but they've still got time to threaten

> rape
>
> castrate
>
> spay you
>
> like a no-good heifer.

I'm not here to settle old scores,
the *run-her-out of-town* history's a territory of memory—

> *jackaroos-bash-the-dykes*
> *pub-night-Friday,*
> *drinking on the highway.*

beef city is a place to test the legislation,
a place to run the plebiscite, the will of the nation, find the free-
speech, no-harm threshold
tap into discussions held in every household

here in the dust of the beef-focussed city,
a bridal party stands up to marry lesbians are seen here faces in the
shadows—
this place of sacred vows

> is the place where you all vote.

I know I'm a dragon in your cat-filled city
I know my frown and fire scares the marble from your beef, in my

high rider boots and flash waistcoat
there are no grooms here no room to normalise your hate.

I know I'm a dragon in your cat-filled city
and all across the country we are waiting for your vote, I know you
are afraid of unleashing pride and difference
there's no room here to normalise your hate.

we don't need a plebiscite, a vote to divide and label us.
we need the politicians to stand and defend us.
we just want equality, change the drift of history
we don't need a plebiscite excuse to raise your hate.

I am a dragon in your dusty cities
a dragon breathing fire melting asphalt on your streets
will the beef-eating people and the cat-filled cities
stand up and call it when we hear the words of hate?

realistically speaking I'll never be on a turned back boat
but I'm a dragon breathing fire, a dragon breathing smoke
I want the politicians to hands up vote.

don't give the hate-sayers reason to harm
accept me as dragon whose time has come—
accept me as a dragon…

she marries her

she asks her for her hand to marry
after five years of not holy espousal nuptial
but partnership in civility *let's do it honey*
promising to waste no time
using her power of eternity
to forgive those of you who voted

on our fit for purpose existence,
you're off the hook for being allowed to
judge us
even those of you who voted NO—
so, buoyed up and serendipitous, Pollyanna-ish—
she marries her

how now, our now?
five years on through viral spreading and un-wealth
social distance gender agenda,
like pushing softly at an open door
were we thinking Utopia, pleasing the world?
she and she are still *a lovely couple*—

brush down our wedding suits
velvet lapels, glossy waistcoats, all the crimson linings
corsages time-withered, concentrating scent and memory
sequential moments of impulsing spontaneity
moth holes a good sign, marking time-moving-on to
jubilance, our tin anniversary

Stigma and structural discrimination against identifying as **LGBTQI+** … highlights bullying, abuse, violence, systemic adversity and negative social and family attitudes'

The Canberra Times, 2021

No place is safe for queer people

When I leave the house I'm in my mask
to save me from your poison breath.
Keeping safe, it is my task.
When I leave the house I'm in my mask,
I know for you it's a lot to ask,
for some of us it's certain death.
When I leave the house I'm in my mask
to save me from your poison breath.

We've known this fear before, remember, in the 80s, when the Grim Reaper scared the hell out of Australia, putting AIDS on the list. And deviant lifestyles, person-to-person sharing of blood and semen, created political quagmire. God's vengeance was brought into it, breath of fire and brimstone. Bowling alleys were never the same, and condoms were front and centre (so to speak) for protection, packed in purses *just in case*… just in case there was resistance to covering up.

No place is safe for queer people. A digressive vagrant, I already require masking for passing, coming out and going out, a cover up, carapace protection from stings and barbs and judgements. Fleeing a place that can kill me has an inevitable inexorability — for queer people being out is always an expected risking.

LGBTQI+ people … treated as scapegoats for the spread of the virus

The Canberra Times, 2021

where bats and queers wear the opprobrium for causing the breakdown of the world order

scientists blame a bat
for bringing the world to its knees
it abandoned the forest and breathed out
scientists blame a bat
we forget we ruined its habitat
bats crowding sunset through trees
scientists blame a bat
for bringing the world to its knees

for fault-lines in the family you blame us queers
loss of the gender binary you're grieving still
in us you see the social order in arrears
for fault-lines in the family you blame us queers
pandemic-fuelled violence makes gender wars clear
name calling won't make us less gay, it might make us ill
for fault-lines in the family you blame us queers
loss of the gender binary you're grieving still

bats fill the sky at sunset, they're awesome
intelligent, remarkable, a keystone species
they're out at night hunting for dinner blossom
bats fill the sky at sunset, they're awesome
before we destroy their habitat, proceed with caution
for their hunting grounds we need co-existence treaties
bats fill the sky at sunset, they're awesome
intelligent, remarkable, a keystone species

it's been quite recent we could voice our dissent,
come out of the closet and come out unmasked
whether gay or queer or trans, we are bent
it's been quite recent we could voice our dissent
your violence against us will it ever relent?
in this pandemic fever we again wear a mask
it's been quite recent we could voice our dissent
come out of the closet and come out unmasked

Part 9: The Last Word

dancing in drag, an anthem for the breakdown of the binary in rondeau

whenever she goes out dancing
in the finery she's currently fancying
she feels the judgement
of all the curmudgeons
who seem to enjoy cancelling

any brownie points gained by abandoning
her boots and comfortable pants
so, she's dancing in drag, the repercussions
         of tomorrow still extant

in heels and dress she begins seeing
her identity rallying, just chancing
to impress on her like an ailment
that stops and starts with her raiment
so, it's out of drag and back to her finery

of waistcoats and boots, with embroidery
to lift it all out of the ordinary
make-up washed off, mask of pigment
        abandoned, tomorrow the drag's non-existent.

Dissenters: We thought never again

In the 60s we were insubordinate, and thought everything, our music
and our freedoms, was new. We were the generation that gave up
fashionable hats, balanced new with second-hand or used, now we're
done with spring, and summer, even autumn; you refer to us as seasons
passed, irretrievable; in our youth we read Sartre, de Beauvoir, Freire
and they prompted us to revolution. Our parents had angst and anger
for our careless rainbow choices; age came on us so suddenly, a shift
from our certainties, held with such belief, unaware of change that
would overwhelm us. We assumed we had access to multiple trajectories
and any reckoning would come later; and so is civilisation, a logical
progression from barbarism to new age, unbroken trajectory of progress
and development, freeing us from arbitrary shifts, from any backward
slide-show to cause us grief. How did we think to change the world,
used as we were to our vote, the weddings, right to work, hate speech
laws? Starting with our revolutions we lived as though it would never
end … all the rainbow colours turning autumn as our ageing passed. We
thought never again the blood-thirsty barbarism of humanity denied, but
now the dark will shock us once again, set the world in shadow, minutes
of silence later, for remembrance, bursting with birdsong, and taut and
tender memories of revolution. So now, how to fight as we were taught
we must, the backlashes, blow back, from the new-lauded ignorance,
just rant and cant. All gains threatened, to be refought every day … so
many borders that were just a shiver have returned in steel, a shocking
shift. The project of our times: protect, defend the thoughtful thinking
of free and educated minds, shift the denigration of intellect, restrictions
on press freedom, dissent invoking incarceration, passed on. We need
the insights of the intelligentsia debating freedoms versus incite-ful
hate-speech used against us. Remember when we thought that all was
won. All rights to education are timely, nothing new. We have always
been the dissidents, resisting hegemony, demanding revolution. Some
smaller things than ignorance may be worth the tumult and the up-swirl
of revolution: China's claim of islands, Russia staking out Crimea and
the moon, all mindset shifts in how the world should run, but avoiding

a return to barbaric brutalism, nothing new — war, slavery, arms sales, abuse of power in all its forms, we can't let them pass us by, incarceration on inhumane detention islands, violence that finds all women, sooner or later... these wicked problems, all require an educated brain be used. Our leaders are completely id, dog whistles, gas-light, sowing doubt, lies, used to redress their perception of missing out and wrongs! We too must reap a revolution, behave in manners inappropriate to our age, that means we fight. It's later than we think, so now we mobilise our aging bones, we're in our petticoats cleaning house, shift as the arc of progress swings a pendulum, back again as if it is new, and passes over, know we are the ark of progress, dissenters, now, who every day carry on the fight anew. Can't save ourselves for later, regret we should have died and strived, and every minute used is not new, thinking that we did our bit but not enough, that the revolution has been and gone with global shifts, and all our lucky golden times have passed!

Notes

p. 3: 'Apostles of Anarchy', *Townsville Daily Bulletin*, 6 July 1978; quoted in Mark Plunkett and Ralph Summy, 'Civil Liberties in Queensland a nonviolent political campaign', *Social Alternatives*, vol. 1, nos 6/7, 1980, p. 87.

p. 4: Paraphrased from call for papers by Jen Webb, *Axon Journal*, 2021.

p. 6: 'On 4 September 1977, in the aftermath of violent clashes between anti-uranium mining demonstrators and police in Sydney, the Premier of Queensland, announced that his government would in future prohibit all street marches in Brisbane other than "recognised non-political processions"', Malcolm Saunders, 'The Civil Liberties Movement in Townsville: 1977-79' in B. J. Dalton (ed.), *Lectures on North Queensland History*, Series 4, Department of History and Politics, James Cook University, Townsville, 1984, fn 1, pp 230-231.

p. 8: Annique Duc and Lee O'Gorman (eds), *Pine Gap – the images: When injustice becomes law resistance becomes duty, Women's Action Against Global Violence* (Women for Survival), Sydney, 1983.

'Apostles of Anarchy', *Townsville Daily Bulletin*, 6 July 1978; quoted in Mark Plunkett and Ralph Summy, 'Civil Liberties in Queensland a nonviolent political campaign', *Social Alternatives*, vol. 1, nos 6/7, 1980, p. 79.

p. 10: Court News, *The Townsville Daily Bulletin*, 11 July 1978.

p. 13: Found poetry with lines taken from 'Police Make a Clean Sweep', *The Townsville Daily Bulletin*, 9 July 1978.

'11 Arrested on Protest March', *The Townsville Daily Bulletin*, 10 July 1978.

p. 20: Extract from Form 17C Number D111281, issued 8 July 1978 at The Right to March demonstration outside the Herbert Hotel in Townsville, Qld.

p. 22 'Nazi Powers for the Police', *The Townsville Daily Bulletin*, Saturday, 3 November 1979.

p. 25: Mark Plunkett, 'Bjelke puts black rights groups under special surveillance', *The National Times*, 21-27 June 1981, p. 13.

p. 32: Jane Cadzow, '"Year of the Lesbian" is the last straw for Susan', *The Australian,* 5 February 1983.

Sylvia da Costa-Roque, 'Year of the Non-existent', *The Courier Mail,* 20 February 1983.

p. 38: 'Women may try to enter Pine Gap', *The Canberra Times,* 10 November 1983.

Janet Wright, 'Women Make a Peace Banner', *The National Times,* 18-24 November 1983, p. 10; 'Inside Pine Gap', *The National Times*, 18-24 November 1983, p. 11.

p. 40: *Human Rights Commission Report*, humanrights.gov.au/sites/default/files/HRC_Report20.doc accessed 5.8.2021.

p. 46-47: Ian McDougall (ed.), 'Poofs in the Park', (Townsville) *Advertiser,* 2 October 1980.

'Beware the Gay Invaders', *The Townsville Advertiser,* 27 September 1984, p. 1.

Tony Koch, '"Homosexual Teachers out", says Powell', *The Courier Mail,* 2 September 1983, p. 1.

Therese Millard, 'Townsville, City of 10,000 gays', *The Townsville Advertiser,* 20 September 1984; '"Homosexuality is perversion" repulsive and sordid says mother of two', *The Townsville Advertiser*, September 1984; Tom Aikens, Townville (MLA Queensland), Letters to the Editor, *Townsville Daily Bulletin,* 17 February 1977; 'a little queer bashing in the Cross', *Lot's Wife,* 30 June 1978; 'Queries on gay teachers', Letters to the Editor, *The Townsville Daily Bulletin,* 22 September 1983; '"Toe the line or be sacked" Joh: Teachers warned on MACOS', *Sunday Mail,* 26 February 1978.

p. 52: George Langley, 'Drink sir, certainly; not deviant, are you?', *The Weekend Australian Magazine,* 9 November 1985.

p. 54: 'World Athletics and FIFA reviewing transgender policies after FINA ruling', ABC News online, 21 June 2022, www.abc.net.au.

p. 58: 'FOUND DEAD IN WOMEN'S CLOTHES', *Central Queensland Herald* (Rockhampton), 18 October 1956, p. 10, accessed online at http:nla.gov.aunla.news-article79270064, 11 May 2021.

pp. 61-62: 'THE MAN IN WOMAN'S CLOTHES', *The Argus* (Melbourne), 23 October 1863, p. 7, accessed online at http:nla.gov.aunla.news-article5737859, 3 November 2020.

A previous version of this poem is published in *Rabbit: a journal for non-fiction poetry*, Issue 34, 2022.

p. 63: Sarah Motherwell, 'Rebel Wilson responds to claims she was outed by '*The Sydney Morning Herald* newspaper', ABC News online, 13 June 2022, www.abc.net.au.

Andrew Hornery, 'I made mistakes over Rebel Wilson, and will learn from them', *The Sydney Morning Herald*, 13 June 2022.

pp. 64-65: This poem is based on selected phrases and words taken from the following article (with help from the Glass Leaves app which I used to randomise the text): Cedric Flower, 'Dressing the part', *The Bulletin*, 89, 18 March 1967, p. 41.

p. 66: *Townsville Daily Bulletin,* 14 September 1983, p. 21.

p. 67: Part I of this piece was published in *Milestones Anthology* (Ginninderra Press, 2021).

pp. 68-69: This poem is based on selected phrases taken from the following article: 'Dykes bashed, no arrests', *Lesbians on the Loose*, 9(12), 1 December 1998, accessed online at http:nla.gov.aunla.obj-1023410286, 5 November 2020.

p. 73: Ben Graham, 'Single post that led to Israel Folau disaster', www.news.com.au/sport/rugby/single-post-that-led-to-israel-folau-disaster/news-story/2074e4f4ea08369d9fe1865453d9abfd, 5 December 2019, accessed 14/8/2021.

Lorde, Audre, 1984, 'History is a weapon: The master's tools will never dismantle the master's house', in *Sister outsider: essays and speeches*, New York: Crossing Press, pp.110-114.

pp. 74-75: Lorde, Audre, 1984, 'History is a weapon: The master's tools will never dismantle the master's house', in *Sister outsider: essays and speeches*, New York Crossing Press, pp.110-114.

p. 76: Alexandra N. Fisher and Michelle K. Ryan, 2021, 'Gender inequalities during COVID-19', *Group Processes & Intergroup Relations*,

24(2), pp. 237–245.

p. 78: Jacob Muñoz, 2021, 'The powerful, complicated legacy of Betty Friedan's *Feminine Mystique*', *Smithsonian Magazine*, www.smithsonianmag.com/smithsonian-institution/powerful-complicated-legacy-betty-friedans-feminine-mystique-180976931/, 4 February 2021, accessed 14/8/2021.

p. 82: Jacob Muñoz, 2021, 'The powerful, complicated legacy of Betty Friedan's *Feminine Mystique*', *Smithsonian Magazine,* www.smithsonianmag.com/smithsonian-institution/powerful-complicated-legacy-betty-friedans-feminine-mystique-180976931/, 4 February 2021, accessed 14/8/2021.

p. 84: Christine Eriksen, 'Building resilience in communities by analysing social dimensions of disaster response', magazine.uow.edu.au, accessed 14/8/2021.

p. 86: Lee Carnie, 'Marriage equality wasn't the end of the fights for equality for LGBTI Australians', 17 May 2018, abc.net.au, accessed 14/8/2021.

p. 88: 'Covid-19 has exposed endemic gender inequality, Guterres tells UN Women's commission', *UN News*, 15 March 2021, news.un.org, accessed 14/8/2021.

p. 90: Harley Dennett, 'Lives in balance while LGBTQI+ stigma remains: PM advisor', *The Canberra Times,* 17 May 2021, www.canberratimes.com.au/profile/1062/harley-dennett, accessed 14/8/2021.

p. 92: Tom McIlroy, 'Canberra tops nation in voting "yes" for same-sex marriage', *The Canberra Times*, 15 November 2017, canberratimes.com.au, accessed 14/8/2021.

In August 2017 The Australian Marriage Law Postal Survey was held to gauge support for legalising same-sex marriage. In effect this allowed every person in the country to vote on whether I was a fit and proper person to be deemed worthy of being included in the polity of the normal. Outrageous! This was a very personal process for me. I felt that every person I came across had been given licence to vote on whether I could join with the mainstream who had rights and freedoms.

'Beef city' previously published in Sandra Renew, *The Orlando Files*, Ginninderra Press, 2018.

p. 95: Previously published online in Red Room Poetry, *30in30*, 2022 Poetry Month, https://redroompoetry.org/poets/sandra-renew/she-marries-her/

p. 96: Harley Dennett, 'Lives in balance while LGBTQI+ stigma remains: PM advisor', *The Canberra Times*, 17 May 2021, www.canberratimes. com.au/profile/1062/harley-dennett, accessed 14/8/2021.

In 1985, 4500 men in inner-suburban Sydney and Melbourne had tested HIV positive. This was person-to-person infections, through blood and semen and other bodily fluids. So far, in 2020, 33 million lives are gone to HIV/AIDS. (Marinella Padula, 'The AIDS Grim Reaper Campaign (A)', The Australia and New Zealand School of Government Case program 2006-90', Australia and New Zealand School of Government, Version 24-11-2008, accessed online at www.anzsog.edu.au, 30 January 2021.)

Previously published in *Not Very Quiet*, issue 8, 2021.

p. 99: Harley Dennett, 'Lives in balance while LGBTQI+ stigma remains: PM advisor', *The Canberra Times*, 17 May 2021, www.canberratimes. com.au/profile/1062/harley-dennett, accessed 14/8/2021.

In 2020 and 2021 the COVID-19 outbreak in Australia was part of an ongoing world-wide pandemic which fundamentally changed the way people viewed their world. Vaccines, border closures, lock downs, masks and social distancing were highly visible functions of how behaviour changed. Perceptions changed too, of the air, of social groups, of entertainment, movement of time and space, our relationship with the animal world.

About the Author

Sandra Renew writes on Ngunnawal and Ngambri land in the heart of Australian national politics, as well as on Yuin country in the presence of Gulaga.

Surviving the 1970s and 1980s in Queensland she continues to write poems that say they are lesbian, and she continues to be fascinated by excesses of power and politics in the main social structures of society.

She lives with her partner and a highly opinionated poodle, and she is her best self in deserts, on road trips and starting the first page of a new notebook.

www.ingramcontent.com/pod-product-compliance
Ingram Content Group Australia Pty Ltd
76 Discovery Rd, Dandenong South VIC 3175, AU
AUHW020639050325
407891AU00002B/5

9 780645 356380